Introduction

The main objective of this book, **updated to 2023**, is to demonstrate the most effective way of formulating the ideal CV. The current job climate in this country at the time of writing is buoyant, with labor shortages in some industries, in particular the service industry. In the legal sector, employers are paying higher salaries to draw in and retain staff.

In the longer term, given the cyclical nature of the economy, it is probable that the jobs market will become more competitive once more, certainly at the professional end, and more people will be chasing fewer jobs.

That's why formulating a CV that stands out from the rest is essential.

Certainly, the way we initially present ourselves to a prospective employer is very important and can mean the difference between getting a job we want and failing. Presenting ourselves begins with the CV. This is the very first contact that an employer will have with us. Although many people know the basics of putting a CV together, there is a big difference between those who have studied the technique and those who have not.

Many applicants undersell themselves right at the outset with a poorly laid out CV that contains too little information. The purpose of this book is to enable those who read it to ensure that the best possible CV is formulated, a CV which shows the applicant in the best light and which provides a steppingstone to the all-important interview. There are numerous ways to 'tweak' a CV, depending on the job that you want to get, or are going for, and there are very good websites around, For example, the University of Kent website www.kent.ac.uk/careers/cv/maturecv.htm which has a host of different styles of CV's tailored to the job that you are going for (and also tips for producing effective CV's). The below is a range of examples that the University offers:

- Chronological CV's (the two examples shown in this book are of the chronological variety).
- Skills based CV's.
- Casual Work CV.
- Creative CV's.
- Law CV's.
- Postgraduate CV's.

Your CV won't actually get you a job!

Whichever type of CV, and approach, you decide to use this may lead you to an interview but won't actually get you the job. This happens at the interview stage. It will, however, get you through the door and put

10

you in the race. Because your CV is so important it is obvious that it should be as neat as possible, presented on good quality paper and accurate in all respects. Remember that your CV is being looked at cold by someone who has never met you and therefore first impressions count for everything.

The book assumes that you will be applying for jobs within the United Kingdom. If this is not the case, you must research the company even more thoroughly and fall in with local customs. For example, in some countries of the world, it is customary to tell the employer in what high esteem you hold them and that you want this job more than any other job. This approach would not be acceptable in the UK. See Chapter 13 for more on this.

The overall approach this book takes is to build up an effective CV as it progresses. It also offers advice to the job hunter in such areas as writing the ideal covering letter and how to construct particular types of CVs depending on your circumstances. application forms, which many firms still insist on, sending your CV ensuring it gets maximum exposure and tips on making it computer friendly are also dealt with.

Throughout this book the masculine gender has been used for ease. However, obviously, the information is for male and female alike.

Good luck with your job hunting!

Section 1

Interpreting Adverts

Ch: 1

Understanding Job Advertisements

If you are sending your CV in response to a job advert, then understanding the job advertisement is the key to designing an effective Curriculum Vitae.

Your CV needs to be formulated with that specific job in mind and it is of fundamental importance that you are able to interpret and analyze the advertisement and make correct deductions. If you do not, then your CV will miss the point and you may not progress to the next stage.

How the job is described

All advertisements will tell the reader the name, location and business of the company. These will be put across in a positive way. Next will come the description. Take time to think about how the job is described. This will enable you to get a real idea of what the company is after. Look to see whether you will be working alone or in a team. This is very important, particularly when emphasizing skills and experience on your CV.

The company will describe what they do, what they require, then go on to outline qualifications and experience required. Obviously, this is one of the most important areas of the advertisement and should be read with care and clearly understood. In some cases, qualifications and experience required will be clearly stated. However, in other cases they won't and it will be up to you to infer these from the advert, based on your knowledge of the job.

Salary

Although, as described above, the salary attached to a job can be misleading, in many cases the actual salary to be offered is not quoted. Statements such as "attractive salary package" or "salary commensurate with age and experience" are employed. The rule here is that if a salary is very attractive it will be quoted. Look at what is said about the salary. The word "circa" may mean 'around' but quite often read by potential applicants as a minimum. Many advertisements, particularly for posts in the public sector, give salary ranges. This shows interested applicants what their potential would be as well as the starting salary. Most organizations will negotiate the starting salary after they have made a decision to employ someone.

Company description and philosophy

Look at what the company has to say for itself. This usually tells you how it wants to perceive itself rather than how others see it. The

16

company may state that it is expanding, or might give that impression by advertising for a number of positions. You might get an idea of the possible promotion prospects from the advertisement. Be wary if there is a lack of company description. This does not always mean that there is a problem, the company may be huge and well known, therefore an in- depth description is not necessary. However, there may well be a flip side and the company may have something to hide, such as concealing recruitment information from other staff.

On company philosophy, look for equal opportunities statements etc. These vary enormously, with the public sector generally leading the way. You need to consider how important the existence of an equal opportunities statement is for you.

Media used to advertise position

The medium used to advertise the post can tell you a lot. If an advertisement is in a national paper then it usually means that the employer has decided that they will spend more money in order to cast their net wider, i.e., nationally instead of locally. Some companies use agencies. This means that they have chosen to have the screening done by another party. In this case, it will be your job to convince the agency that they should introduce you to the company. Sometimes, the agency carries out initial interviews and only submits the short list to their client. You may want to consider making your application more general if the agency handles many jobs in the industry in which you work. Think about the reasons why the organizations use agencies. Do they want specialists for expertise in that area themselves? This can be true when companies are seeking personnel at the top of a department, where there is nobody above with the kind of knowledge required to recruit that person.

Good advertisements are not only the right size but are also the right shape too. They have usually been professionally designed to attract the reader to the text, demonstrating careful planning and thought. Not all organizations can afford this approach. Look for simple indicators too, i.e., is the advertisement boxed? Lineage advertisements in local papers may tell you that the company is small and unsophisticated in terms of recruitment. Look at how accurately the job is described - beware of those sounding too good to be true, few jobs live up to this.

The above are key things to look out for when reading a job advertisement. Remember, read the advertisement carefully; concentrate on each aspect building up a picture as you go. If you are in any doubt, contact the company advertising the job and request further information.

Now read the key points from Chapter One.

KEY POINTS FROM CHAPTER ONE

- Pay careful attention to the job description in the advertisement. This will enable you to get a clear idea of what the company wants.

- Most organizations will negotiate the starting salary after they have made a decision to employ someone

- Read the company description carefully and try to determine the company philosophy

- The medium used by the organization to advertise the post will tell you a lot about the organization

- If the company uses an agency, you may want to structure your CV a little differently.

**

Section 2

Compiling Your CV

Ch: 2

Putting Together a CV

Having either decided to send out your CV to various employers or websites, or CV banks (see later) or examined and analyzed a job advertised, you should now be in a position to begin constructing your CV.

Fundamental requirements of a CV

The letters "CV" stand for Curriculum Vitae, which derives from Latin. Translated, this means "the way your life has run". Correspondingly, the CV is a personal statement, which demonstrates to the employer the way your life has run. The CV will usually start from your early education and progress through to higher education and chronicle your employment. It will also chronicle your personal interests. The end product should present a well-rounded picture of you.

A CV serves several basic requirements. Firstly, it highlights your potential value to an employer. It also provides a framework within which an interview can be guided and acts as a record of the interview, or its substance. Many people suffer mental blocks when required to formulate a CV. It can be hard work. Time and effort plus creativity are key components of the task. The most important point to remember at the outset is that the CV should be concise and easy to read. All of the relevant and most important facts should be present.

The layout of the ideal CV

Before any information has been entered onto the CV, consideration needs to be given to the layout. By layout, I mean the actual design of the visual presentation. Remember that a better impression will be made if the person reading the CV feels comfortable with what they are reading. Effective visual design reflects neatness, and the end product should be easy on the eyes and immediately give an impression of orderliness, which will go a long way to impress the reader.

Chapter Seven gives two examples of complete CV's laid out in a simple but effective manner.

Although final recruitment decisions are not made on visual presentation alone, as opposed to content, the way information is assembled makes an important first impression and could mean the difference between someone bothering to spend time with your CV or deciding to move on to the next one.

Make sure also when you are typing the information that you use all of the features of the Word Processor (assuming that you are using a WP). Make sure that you have clean margins and that you are

24

consistent when presenting your information. For example, you might want to ensure that your work is not right hand justified as this lends a certain uniformity to a CV. Maybe it is better to leave it unjustified or "ragged right" as it is known. You should also consider the font that you are using.

Fonts

TIMES NEW ROMAN is the standard windows "serif" font. A safe bet - law firms seem to like it but it isn't easy to read on the screen, especially in the small font size you may need to use to get your CV on one or two pages. If you do prefer to use a serif font, try CAMBRIA which has been designed for screen readability. See the example fonts to the right to see how much clearer Cambria looks than Times New Roman.

Classier choices might be VERDANA or LUCIDA SANS which have wider letters than most fonts but, if you are running out of space, then Arial is more space saving, as is TAHOMA which is a narrower version of Verdana. Notice how, in the example to the right, Verdana looks bigger and easier to read than Times New Roman. CALIBRI is now the standard MS Word font but is smaller and perhaps less clear than Arial, Verdana or Lucida Sans

FONT SIZE is normally 12 points for the normal font with larger sizes for subheadings and headings.

Most CVs are now read on screen rather than on paper. It's no coincidence that Serif fonts are rarely used on the web - they are much less readable on screen and some fonts, such as Verdana, were designed with screen readability in mind. The CV examples set out in this book are in Adobe Garamond, which is another popular font.

Quality

Obviously the quality of a CV depends very much on the way it is laid out and the information contained within it. However, it is also true to say that a much better impression is made with a quality paper. There are different qualities and thickness of paper and I would recommend that a thicker more durable paper be used, such as Conqueror. A good quality paper at the outset enhances the effort that you will make when laying out information and presenting yourself in the best light.

Style

By style, I am referring to the way you present information about yourself. Remember that there are two important rules underlying any form of presentation. Be brief and be clear! You do not want to bore the reader by going on and on, using twenty words when five will do. However, conversely, you do not want to be too brief and exclude the main emphasis of what you wish to get across. Writing the ideal CV is a skilled business and requires thought and

26

concentration, along with creative editing. If possible, I would advise showing the finished product to someone skilled in the art of report writing before you send it to a prospective employer. As we progress through the book there will be examples of the kind of style you should be aiming for. These examples will build up into a complete CV, which should set the standard you are trying to achieve.

The basic structure

Although the basic structure of a CV is well known, it is more important to structure the CV in a way that shows you in the best light. The traditional (chronological) structure of a CV is as follows:

Name

Address

Occupation

Telephone number (landline and mobile)

Email

Date of birth (optional)

Place of birth

Marital status

Next of kin

Health

Driving license

Religion (if applicable)

National insurance number (optional)

(Sometimes religion, nationality and passport number if applying for a job abroad)

Secondary education

Higher education

Professional qualifications

Employment history

Other (interests, achievements etc.)

There are several variants on this approach. Remember, what you are doing is delivering information to the potential employer. This person might well be interested in your employment history at the outset and it may be more effective to deliver this information right at the beginning. Leave the matter of details such as date of birth and secondary education until the end and begin with the most important first. Therefore, instead of adopting the traditional approach you might want to use the following format:

Name

Address

Telephone number

Email

Career

Achievements

Professional qualifications

Education

Interests

Other personal details

Date of birth

We have considered the most important aspects of the ideal CV. These are quality, style and layout. Finally, there is the content. These initial pointers should enable you to begin to put together your first CV. In the following chapter we will look at the presentation of your personal details and how to obtain the ideal structure. It is important to remember that I will be following the traditional format when presenting each area of information. It will be up to yourself to rearrange the format as you think best.

Now read the key points from Chapter Two overleaf.

**

KEY POINTS FROM CHAPTER TWO

DESIGNING THE IDEAL CV

■ Your CV should always present a well-rounded, balanced picture of you as a person.

■ Your CV highlights your potential value to an employer. It should be concise and easy to read

■ Your CV should be well laid out. Visual presentation is of the utmost importance

■ Use good quality paper when producing your CV.

■ Be brief and clear when outlining the various areas of your CV.

■ Use a tried and tested format. There are several variations outlined in this book.

**

Ch: 3

Your Personal Details

The approach from here on is to build up a complete CV, with each chapter concentrating on a specific area. As I stated in Chapter Two, personal details do not necessarily come first in your CV but the arrangements of this section are similar in all CVs. The only differences relate to the amount of information given and where it appears. The most obvious information you should open with is that of your name and address and telephone number. You should also put your occupation.

Date of birth and place of birth

If the CV is being assembled for a single job application then the applicant's age should appear alongside the date of birth. This reduces the reading time of the CV. When the CV is to be used over a long period then the date of birth should be inserted because the passage of time will lead to inaccuracy. The entry giving details about ages of children can also become outdated and therefore it is important to supply date of birth here too. In addition to date of birth, place of birth should be entered too. Interestingly, many public sector employers now do not ask for date of birth on application forms, as the feeling is that this may lead to indirect discrimination when picking a candidate. However, it is the norm to do so on CV's.

Nationality

Depending on what post you are applying for, and where in the world, you should refer to nationality. If the job is in the United Kingdom, this is not strictly necessary.

Religion

Again, you should only make reference to religion if it is relevant. For most job applications, it is not necessary. For jobs abroad where it is deemed to be of importance you should state your religion.

Marital status

Make reference to whether you are married or single. It is not really necessary to allude to the fact that you are separated or divorced.

Next of kin

Next of kin should be entered as a matter of course, particularly if the nature and type of work is dangerous.

Passport number

You should make reference to this if the post is abroad. Otherwise it is not necessary. Note the comments about identity fraud overleaf.

Health

Another sub-heading which may not be used in all instances is that of health. This will apply if physical fitness is an important consideration, jobs such as swimming instructor, physical fitness trainer etc.

Driving license

Details concerning your driving license can be important. A potential employer may be impressed by a clean license. If the license is not clean then you should indicate that you have a full license only. However, as with the passport number, taken note of the comments concerning identity fraud overleaf.

Relocation

If you wish it to be known that you would be prepared to relocate to another part of the country then you should indicate this. You may not want to be specific here, therefore leaving open the question of relocation.

National insurance number

Your national insurance number should always be included in your personal details. This is particularly relevant when the CV is being used to apply for a job offshore. You should know your own field of work and when to include this information. Personal details should be presented as in the example below. You may not require all of the information outlined. However, it is important to remember that you are tailoring your details to the potential employer. Obviously, some of the details will be wholly dependent on your prospective employer.

PERSONAL DETAILS	
Full Name:	Rupert James
Occupation:	Computer Scientist
Address:	92 Faversham Street Weybridge Surrey
Telephone Number:	01239 6789
Mobile	98767545321
Email	info@straightforwardbooks.co.uk
Date of Birth:	5-3-93
Place of Birth:	Rich Street Ninetown Anywhere
Nationality:	British
Religion:	Buddhist
Marital Status:	Married with son aged 7
Next of Kin:	Mrs. James address as above

National ins no:	To be provided.
Driving License:	Current full
Passport Number:	Full British passport.
Health:	Excellent
Preferred location:	Anywhere at all

The personal details section of the CV is straightforward. The most important point to remember is that apart from the obvious information, such as name and address there are important areas which are directly relevant to the job for which you are applying and which you must include.

Be mindful about identity fraud!

You should be aware, when filling in personal details, that you may be exposed to an increased risk of identity fraud. It is a fact that 50% of CV's contain enough personal information to enable an identity fraudster to successfully apply for a credit card.

The most useful information is the most basic information, such as address and date of birth. marital status is also very useful. A national insurance number is also very useful.

The main message only include the most relevant details, it is not necessary to expose your self to the whole world.

Now read the key points from Chapter Three overleaf.

KEY POINTS FROM CHAPTER THREE
PRESENTATION OF PERSONAL DETAILS

■ Your personal details may vary according to the post offered

■ If your CV is being assembled for a single job application, mention your age. For multiple applications mention your date of birth

■ Don't forget to include your name and address. Many people do!

**

Ch: 4

Education, Qualifications and Training

Obviously, education, qualifications and training will differ according to individual experience. Normally, in a CV you would include education from the age of eleven onwards. It is not necessary to include schools attended prior to secondary schools. Sometimes a person will have attended more than one secondary school, for a variety of reasons, such as parents moving job, and in this case you should normally only include the last two schools.

Your achievements at school, in the form of GCSE should be clearly demonstrated. You might wish to emphasize the most relevant passes first although it is usual to rank the passes in descending order.

Example

JULY 2009

GCSE

English	Grade (d)
Biology	(c)
French	(c)
Physics	(c)
Economics	(a)

And so on.

Higher Education

For those who have received an education after leaving secondary school, whether it is university or technical college, it is usual to present the nature and type of education and your qualifications. For those who left school and went straight into employment with no formal qualifications it is usual to proceed with your career history. If you have gone on to higher education then the next stage of the CV will look something like this:

September 2012-July 2016 Waldesley Polytechnic High Street Waldesley

Subject BA Computer Sciences Grade   2.1

If your further education has been more technically oriented, i.e., part time day release, then the entry would look more like this:

September 2012 - September 2016 City and Guilds

Subject	Computer Science Part 1
Grade	Pass

September 2016 - September 2017 City and Guilds

Subject	Computer Science Part 2
Grade	Pass with merit

38

The above is only an example and does not relate to the actual computing syllabus. It could be that you have attained a number of qualifications during your time at university or college and that you have a long list of diplomas or certificates. The question to consider here is whether or not to include them all or whether to stick to the relevant ones.

The employer would first and foremost be interested in the qualification, which is most relevant to the job being applied for. Then the focus would be on the relevant areas of practical experience underpinning the paper qualification. Although you may have obtained numerous certificates or diplomas in other subjects, which may well be an indication of intelligence, self-discipline and determination, it is really the most relevant qualification, which is the most important. The key point to remember is that information overload may serve as a distraction and draw the potential employer's attention away from the most important qualification.

Placements during training

Placements with other organizations, such as industrial placements or college placements, whatever the length should be treated as a normal job in the career history, with the placement clearly emphasized:

Example

October 2012 - April 2013   Finetronics Ltd, Long Road, Waldesley.

Computer Trainee - Assisting the Chief Engineer
on placement developing computer systems

Short courses

Over the years an applicant will have attended many short courses either connected with his employment or voluntarily. You should only really make reference to short courses if they have relevance to the job being applied for. Again it is no use entering a proliferation of courses attended if all you are achieving is information overload.

Example

Authentic Electronics Ltd

July (2017) Fault finding on Computers (2 days)

September (2017)   Software Analysis

December (2017)   Advanced Spreadsheets

Sometimes recruitment agencies will rely on key words when retrieving potential candidates from databases. For example, Comp for computer specialists. If your CV is going to a particular agency it is a good idea to ensure that you are aware of the need to insert any relevant abbreviations, which might be used as key words

40

.Professional Associations

It is at this point, at the end of your formal qualifications and before your career history, that you would insert your professional qualifications, if any. Professional qualifications, in most cases, are obtained following a specialist course and then after a period in the relevant job. A professional qualification is intended to demonstrate that you have received the appropriate amount of academic and practical training and that you are a competent person able to operate in your given field. Therefore, the entry might look like this:

Professional Association: Royal Institution of Computer Technicians. Date entered: October 2017

If you think it is relevant, you might consider using the letters relating to your profession alongside your name when entering your personal details. The same consideration might also be given to Educational qualifications, i.e. BA (hons).

Service in the Armed Forces

If you have served in the Armed Forces then your education within the military will be emphasized in exactly the same way as the previous example. The potential employer will see at a glance that you were in the forces and will expect to see this in your career history.

Education, Training and Qualifications

Building up on what we have included so far, this section of your CV should look as follows:

Education: 2004-2010

Northampton Grammar School

GCE Passes:

English   Grade (d)

Biology   (c)

French   (c)

Physics   (b)

Economics   (b)

Higher Education

2010-2014 Waldesley Polytechnic, High Street, Waldesley

Northampton

BA   Computer Sciences: Pass with distinction

Year One: Computer Theory

Year Two: Advanced Computer Theory

"   "   Computer Trainee on placement,

ElectronicsSystems Ltd, Long Road, Northampton. Assisting the Chief Engineer developing computer systems

Year Three: Applied Computing

Short Courses

Authentic Electronics Limited

July 2017   Fault-finding on Computers (2 days)

September 2017   Software Analysis (1 week)

December 2017   Advanced Spreadsheets (1 week)

Professional Association

Royal Institute of Computer Scientists

Fellow of the Institute October 2017

Now read the key points from Chapter Four overleaf.

**

KEY POINTS FROM CHAPTER FOUR
EDUCATION, QUALIFICATIONS AND TRAINING

■ Include only education from the age of eleven onwards (secondary)

■ Your achievements at school should be clearly demonstrated

■ Highlight higher education. Emphasize your most relevant qualifications

■ Emphasize relevant short courses

■ Be aware of the need to insert relevant abbreviations when sending your CV to recruitment agencies

■ Highlight professional associations to which you belong

■ Highlight service in the Armed Forces

**

Ch: 5

Career History

So far we have looked at personal details and your education and qualifications. However, it is true to say that it is the next part of your CV which will be of the most interest to the would-be employer.

This section, of all sections, will demand the greatest amount of time and thought, as employers will be looking to see what sort of experience you can bring to their organization. Although your education may be first class and your qualifications second to none they will almost always take second place to your actual experience in a particular field.

When producing this area of the CV (as with all areas) avoid long flowing prose and avoid the use of the first person, i.e., I \ we, as your document will only usually get a quick first reading and therefore lots of irrelevant information may put off the potential employer. Familiarity in a CV will usually go down very badly indeed so stick to the facts and be objective.

You should always begin with your current employer first (or most recent) devoting the most time and space here, as it is the one the potential employer will see as most relevant. The standard procedure is to catalogue your jobs in reverse order, showing the name and business of the employer, the dates of employment in months and years and the job and duties.

The material must be well organized in this section to enable the employer to see where your main strengths are. The exact address of the organization is not needed but is helpful to indicate the area. Some people do not name their company. This is not recommended. It gives the impression that they are ashamed of it and makes it harder for the person assessing the application to get a feel for what the individual was doing.

Many things are deduced by the reader, taking into account the job title, the company business and size and the list of your duties. These things all contribute to helping to build up a picture of the sort of work undertaken and leaving out the company name denies the reader some of that information.

You will not need to give details of the grades of your previous positions. This would be irrelevant to a new employer and in any case the recruiter is unlikely to know the details of the grading structure of your last employers. Although you may have been in a high grade, omit details of this. Ensure instead that you put in information on any promotions that you gained. You may also want to mention merit increases gained, although this may be done through the covering letter rather than the curriculum vitae. In cases where you have undertaken a number of similar jobs, amalgamate these into one section if this is feasible. Give a brief outline of the duties with the caveat that you had similar employment in those companies and give inclusive dates.

You do not have to include reasons for leaving, or salary. However, you might want to indicate the salary for your current/last employment in order to give the prospective employer an indication of what salary you might be asking for.

Your career history

Taking into account the above, the section of your CV dealing with your career history would look as follows:

CAREER HISTORY

August 2022 - current.

Authentic Computers, Northampton. Consultant

In this post, I am acting in the capacity of consultant to the private and public sectors, advising on systems usage. I am employing the technical know how gained in my previous jobs.

I am conversant with most computer packages

Salary: £25,000 Per Annum

September 2018 - July 2022

London Borough of Shepwhich. Senior Computer Manager

In this post, I had responsibility for overseeing a change in the authority's computer system. This involved carrying out systems analysis and producing a brief for the council, who subsequently accepted the brief and instructed the computer department to effect the change.

After two years I was promoted from Computer Manager to Senior Computer Manager.

September 2017 - August 2018

I took one year out before work to fulfill ambitions to travel around the world with my wife.

Now read the key points from Chapter Five overleaf.

**

KEY POINTS FROM CHAPTER FIVE

PRESENTATION OF CAREER DETAILS

■ This section of your CV is the most important area of the Document

■ Avoid long flowing prose. Avoid the use of the first person

■ Begin with your current employer first, listing jobs in reverse order

**

Ch: 6

Additional Information

In addition to the main points of your C.V, you may feel that it is necessary to include other details. The following covers main areas of information that may assist the interviewer in the initial stages of the job-hunting process.

Health

Unless you have had a serious illness that you feel a potential employer should be aware of, then it might be wise to omit this. The person scrutinizing the application will assume that you are in good health unless you state otherwise. If you have spent time away from employment due to illness, and there is a gap in your CV. then it might be wise to explain this separately, emphasizing that there are no recurring problems and that you are fit for work.

References

Omit references unless you are specifically asked for them. Where you are asked to give references, use your most recent or current employer if possible and the one immediately prior to that. If you are applying for your first job, be prepared to use a tutor at your school or college. Whenever you give the name of referees, ask the individuals first if they are willing to provide a reference for you.

Salary

This is another detail that can generally be omitted, especially if your employment history spans a few years. Payments received several decades ago are not relevant now. The employer is more interested in your most recent salary, as they will usually base their own decisions on this information. If your salary is good in your current job, you may want to leave details of this out as it may deter a potential employer of they think that they cannot match it. If your current salary is poor, the reader may wish to know why this is the case. Therefore, you may wish to leave this blank also.

Personal Interests

You should think carefully about what you wish to include in this section. Try to tailor it to the post you are applying for. Try to list interests that show a balance. A healthy interest in sport and the outdoors should be counterbalanced by other, more intellectual pursuits. In general, keep this section short, as it is an extra, which you are adding in order to give the reader a more complete picture of you.

Languages

You should make reference to languages that you can speak, other than your mother tongue, only if they are pertinent to the post applied for. Only give information about languages that you can speak if you really know them. It is no good embellishing the truth and being shown up at an interview.

Other

Make reference to your driving license. Usually, employers like to see that you have a license although some jobs do not require one. If you have produced any publications that are relevant to the post, make reference to these. Generally, it is the more academically inclined jobs that feel publications are relevant. However, other employers offering legal or advice posts might be suitably impressed if you have produced work that has been published. Experience in the Armed Forces usually impresses employers as it denotes a person who has been subject to a life of organized discipline and would probably turn out to be a trustworthy employee. This, of course, may not always be the case, but general perceptions are most important when getting beyond the first stage.

**

Section 3

The Complete CV

Ch: 7

Examples of Complete CV's

The following are examples of two different layout styles of a CV. The information is the same and includes all elements. However, you should include and exclude information depending on the perceived requirements of the employer. For example, it may not be necessary to include religion or location or other facts. This depends entirely on the employer.

Example 1

PERSONAL DETAILS

Full Name:	Rupert James
Occupation:	Computer Scientist
Address:	92 Faversham Street
Telephone No:	012396789
Mobile	98767545321
Email	info@straightforwardcbooks.co.uk
Date of Birth:	5-3-93
Place of Birth:	Rich Street Ninetown Anywhere
Nationality:	British
Religion:	Buddhist

Marital Status:	Married with son aged 2
Next of Kin:	Mrs James address as above
National ins no:	123456789
Driving License:	Current full
Passport Number:	456789
Health:	Excellent
Preferred location:	Anywhere at all

Education, Training and Qualifications

Education: 2004 - 2010

Northampton Grammar School

GCE Passes:

English	Grade (d)
Biology	(c)
French	(c)
Physics	(b)
Economics	(b)

Higher Education

2011 - 2014 Waldesley Polytechnic, High Street,

Waldesley Northampton

BA Computer Sciences: Pass with distinction

Year One:	Computer Theory
Year Two	Advanced Computer Theory
"	Computer Trainee on placement,
	ElectronicsSystems Ltd,
	Long Road, Northampton.
	Assisting the Chief Engineer
	developing computer systems

Year Three: Applied Computing

Short Courses

Authentic Electronics Limited September 2022 Fault finding on Computers (2days)

October 2022	Software Analysis (1 week)
December 2022	Advanced Spreadsheets (1 week)

Professional Association

Royal Institute of Computer Scientists

Fellow of the Institute May 2017

CAREER HISTORY

August 2022 - current.

Authentic Electronics, Northampton. Consultant

In this post, I am acting in the capacity of consultant to the private and public sectors, advising on systems usage. I am employing the technical know how gained in my previous jobs.

I am conversant with most computer packages
Salary: £25,000 Per Annum

September 2018 - July 2022
London Borough of Shepwhich. Senior Computer Manager
In this post, I had responsibility for overseeing a change in the authority's computer system. This involved carrying out systems analysis and producing a brief for the council, who subsequently accepted the brief and instructed the computer department to effect the change.

After two years I was promoted from Computer Manager to Senior Computer Manager.

Whilst employed by The London Borough of Shepwhich I obtained the status of Fellow of the Royal Institute of Computer Scientists. My main duties for the company were to oversee the development of a computer system for a local authority. This involved giving technical advice to the authority and supervising a workforce of 23 people who were directly involved in the installation of the equipment. During this time, I gained experience of the following packages:

Wing 1 - Wing 2 - Super Wing-Wing for Windows

September 2017 - August 2018

I took two years out from work to fulfill ambition to travel around the world with my wife.

Personal Interests

I am interested in squash, badminton and indoor football. In addition, I am interested in studying history and Science. I enjoy walking in the countryside and swimming. I also like to participate in the community and am on the local conservation committee. I speak French and German fluently and have traveled to these countries for my current employer on business.

Health

Excellent

Preferred location

London

Example 2

Name   Rupert James

Address   92 Faversham Street Weybridge Surrey

Telephone number   020 8 1234 5678

Mobile   98767545321

Email info@straightforwardco.co.uk

Occupation   Computer Scientist

Career

August 2022 - current.

Authentic Electronics, Northampton. Consultant

In this post, I am acting in the capacity of consultant to the private and public sectors, advising on systems usage. I am employing the technical know how gained in my previous jobs.

I am conversant with most computer packages

Salary: £25,000 Per Annum

September 2018 - July 2022

London Borough of Shepwhich. Senior Computer Manager

In this post, I had responsibility for overseeing a change in the authority's computer system. This involved carrying out systems analysis and producing a brief for the council, who subsequently accepted the brief and instructed the computer department to effect the change.

After two years I was promoted from Computer Manager to Senior Computer Manager.

Whilst employed by The London Borough of Shepwhich I obtained the status of Fellow of the Royal Institute of Computer Scientists. My main duties for the company were to oversee the development of a computer system for a local authority. This involved giving technical advice to the authority and supervising a workforce of 23 people who were directly involved in the installation of the equipment. During this time, I gained experience of the following packages:

Wing 1 - Wing 2 - Super Wing-Wing for Windows

September 2017 – August 2018
I took one year out from work to fulfill ambition to travel around the world with my wife.

Professional Qualifications
Fellow of the Royal Institute of Computer Scientists, May 2017.

Education, Training and Qualifications

Education: 2004 - 2010

Northampton Grammar School

GCE Passes:

English   Grade (d)

Biology   (c)

French   (c)

Physics   (b)

Economics   (b)

Higher Education

2011–2014   Waldesley   Polytechnic,   High   Street,   Waldesley
Northampton

BA   Computer Sciences: Pass with distinction

Year One: Computer Theory

Year Two: Advanced Computer Theory

          Computer Trainee on placement,

          Electronics   Systems   Ltd,   Long   Road,   Northampton.
Assisting the Chief Engineer developing computer systems

Year Three: Applied computing

Short Courses

Authentic Electronics Limited

July 2017	Fault finding on Computers (2 days)
October 2017	Software Analysis (1 week)
December 2017	Advanced Spreadsheets (1 week)

Personal Interests

I am interested in squash, badminton and indoor football. In addition, I am interested in studying history and Science. I enjoy walking in the countryside and swimming. I also like to participate in the community and am on the local conservation committee. I speak French and German fluently and have traveled to these countries for my current employer on business.

Other personal details

Date of Birth:	5-3-93
Place of Birth:	Rich Street Ninetown Anywhere
Nationality:	British
Religion:	Buddhist
Marital Status:	Married with Son aged 2
Next of Kin:	Mrs. Smith address as above
National ins no:	012396789
Driving License:	Current full

Passport Number:	456789
Health:	Excellent
Preferred location:	Anywhere at all

The above two examples represent two different ways of laying out a CV. The information is the same but is presented in a different way. The reader will see different facts first. You must decide which will be of primary importance for this particular employer. The key point is that you are presenting what you consider to be the most important and relevant facts first.

Example one concentrated on personal details first, followed by education and career Example two-placed immediate emphasis on career then education, with personal details last.

**

Ch: 8

Different CV's

As mentioned in the introduction to this book, the University of Kent has a very good website with a range of different CV styles, suitable to the job that you will be going for. Their site is www.kent.ac.uk/careers/cv/cvexamples. Below are a few tips for other groups.

School leavers

Most school leavers will have very little experience of the job market, with the exception of a Saturday job or evening employment. The fact that you do not have a career history to demonstrate should enable you to keep this part of your CV brief. Generally, you should aim to keep to one side of A4 paper.

Your education will be the most important part of your CV if you are a school leaver. You should try to include any work experience that you may have had. This will include work experience programmes and Youth Training Programmes. You should list all work experience, highlighting grades achieved. If they are not too good, you should omit them. The employer can ask for details if these are needed. You will invariably have to explain the nature of the qualifications. If you are older then the school system will have changed. However, if you are about to leave school then the would-be employer may not understand your qualifications. One example is that employers are now getting used to the grading systems of the GCSE and General National Vocational Qualifications) and would possibly be out of touch or not see the relevance of GCSE levels. You should attempt to make a connection between your hobbies and your personal qualities, which show your skills and aptitudes. Organizational skills are generally valued and participation in voluntary work can help to create a positive image of you as a person.

Do try to avoid quoting too many interests or give the impression of being a flighty person. The employer is usually more concerned that you are able to settle into a work environment, especially as you have not experienced the world of work and the attendant discipline.

If you are a graduate and have been involved in the arena of student politics, be careful how you mention this. Some employers are not over keen to employ someone who they perceive may cause disruption or upset a well-established applecart. There is no harm mentioning areas of responsibility such as president of your branch of the National Union of Students, but don't go much beyond this, unless of course a prospective employer knows you and your political skills and history are an asset.

Graduates

For those people who are just graduating, or have graduated, obviously the emphasis will be on experience at University or College. However, the whole emphasis won't be on the academic content but will also be on what you did outside of your studies, such as vacation work, gap year and so on.

What you need to illustrate is that you are self-disciplined, have goals in life and also have initiative. This is likely to get you to the interview stage in your chosen career path.

The key is to structure your CV in such a way that you start with personal details and then, after early schooling, build up the years that you were a student and bring out all aspects of your experience and use this to justify your choice of job and why you are applying for a particular job.

Long Term Unemployed

If you have never been employed, or it has been many years since you were in employment, the main problem that you will find is explaining the gap in your employment, and demonstrating that you are still employable. At all costs you must avoid giving the prospective employer the impression that you feel hard done by or have a chip on your shoulder.

Employers want to take on positive employees, not those disgruntled and harboring past resentments. At the end of the day, you have a selling job to do and it will be no easy task to convince the employer that you are ready to re-enter the world of work.

Redundancy

If you have been made redundant, try to show that you understand the company's reasons behind the re-organization. If the organization went out of business, try to show that your attitude towards this was responsible. And do not let the reader of the CV think that this was in any way due to you. Show that you have somehow learned from the experience by doing something positive which will help you in your future career. If you have undertaken formal training to prepare for a career change or advancement, be specific in how that training fitted the job applied for in the new company.

If you are circulating many unsolicited applications, you must still tailor these to the organizations and the kinds of jobs that you are interested in. Your application is wasted without this. In unsolicited applications, ask if they have any current vacancies for the sort of post that you are seeking. Ask whether their future planning indicates that there may be any available in the near future. Remember to include your most positive points, including the ability to work immediately. This can be a very valuable plus point in your application. .

Career Breaks

If you have had a career break to raise a family, for example, or are changing career direction it can be very difficult to convince a prospective employer that you are serious about the post and are committed to it. You must convince the employer that you are firmly committed to working and that you have a real interest in their field of work. Cite any refresher courses that you any have taken and emphasize that your childcare arrangements are adequate.

Your career change may be due to circumstances beyond your control. If you have undertaken retraining, sound positive about this and indicate that it was thorough and that you took it seriously. If you are returning to work after a spell in prison, note the Rehabilitation of Offenders Act 1974. This covers people with certain past convictions, but who have not been convicted again for specific lengths of time. After these trouble free periods, the individuals are deemed to have spent their convictions and do not have to declare them. If the conviction has no bearing on your prospective employment and you can avoid mentioning it you should do so. However, you must not lie about it and may have to declare it if asked.

If you are returning to employment in the United Kingdom after working abroad, you must show how the position you held abroad was similar to the kind of job that you had here. The recruiter must be convinced that the change in culture would not mean that your training and abilities have a completely different slant. You may be able to stress the positive side of this too, emphasizing your increased awareness of the international business scene. If you have worked overseas, references may be difficult for the employer to follow up. Testimonials, translated as necessary, may be useful in this situation.

Now read the key points from Chapter Eight overleaf.

**

KEY POINTS FROM CHAPTER EIGHT
OTHER C.V'S

■ If you are a school leaver, keep your CV brief and to the point

■ Your education will be the most important part of the CV

■ Make a connection between your hobbies and your personal qualities. Try to avoid quoting too many personal interests

■ If you are a graduate emphasize your experience (if any) other than your academic experience

■ If you are long term unemployed, try to avoid giving the impression that you are disgruntled or resentful

■ If you have been made redundant try to portray the redundancy in a positive light. If you have undertaken formal training since being made redundant, be specific in how that training fits the job applied for

■ If you have had a career break, you must convince the prospective employer that you are now fully committed to returning to work.

Section 4
Covering Letters

Ch: 9
The Ideal Covering Letter

A covering letter with your CV is really a letter of introduction and is usually the first thing that a prospective employer reads. You should always send a covering letter with a CV or application form. If your application is speculative this is even more important.

The reason for sending the letter is to make sure that the prospective employer has all the facts. Make sure that you keep a copy of what you send.

Rules of letter writing

Ensure that you use a good quality paper, ideally A4 so that it fits well with other documentation. Do not use colored paper with elaborate designs.

Your letter can be word processed or handwritten as long as the end result is that it is legible. If a person cannot read your letter then they will dispose of it, along with your CV. If you know that your handwriting is bad then word-process the letter. Use black ink for writing letters as this makes it easier for photocopying. The usual rules of spelling and grammar apply in letters as they do in the CV.

The overall effect has to convince the reader that they are dealing with a professional.

Any letter that you send must be formal. It must be well set out and show respect to the person that you are writing to. Remember, if you start the letter by saying Dear Sir you must end by saying 'yours faithfully' and that if you use the persons name you must end with 'yours sincerely'. Note that the 'f' and the 's' are in the lower case.

Note how the title of the recipient is given in the advert. If the text asks you to reply to a specific person then you should do just that. Always address the person by their surname and never their forename.

Put your address in the top right hand corner of the letter. You should not put your own name here but leave it until the end of the letter, where you will print and sign. You can, if necessary, put your telephone number under your address. If you put the name and address of the recipient, this should be further down the page on the left hand side. Depending on your style of letter, this date can either be beneath your own address or under the recipients address.

Space the letter out as well as you can. Again, the main rule of letter writing is that the recipient has to get a clear impression of the writer. The more legible the letter, the better laid out, the better the impression. If the letter is short, such as a letter requesting an application form then you should start further down the page. If there is lots of information in the letter, then you should commence higher up the page. If you can possibly fit it all on one side, then all the better.

Below, you will see an example of a letter forwarding a CV to a prospective employer. Following this, you will see a further two examples. The first one is requesting an application form. The second is returning an application form to a prospective employer.

EXAMPLE 1 OVERLEAF

Example 1

Daniel Green

Raft Enterprises

Codley Way

Northampton

N1 F45

1st October any date

92 Faversham Street

Weybridge

Surrey

Tel: 020 8123 6789

Dear Mr. Green

Your Ref: ABCDEFG. Vacancy for a Computer Scientist.

I would like to apply for the position of computer scientist with your company. I saw the advertisement in the Times in 9th September any date.

As you will see from my enclosed CV, I have been a computer manager since I graduated from Northampton University in 1996. I have been involved in the public and private sectors, overseeing systems analysis and installation.

I believe that I have the experience that you are seeking and would be very interested in working for Raft Enterprises. I look forward to hearing from you.

Yours sincerely

Rupert James

Example 2

92 Faversham Street

Weybridge

Surrey

John Baldrick

Tel: 0208 123 6789

Baldrick Enterprises

Jones Street

Northamption

N1 4RG

1st October any date.

Dear Mr. Baldrick

Your ref: COMP 123. Computer Manager

I am responding to your advertisement in the Times newspaper for a computer scientist. Could you please forward me an application form.

I look forward to hearing from you.

Yours sincerely

Rupert James

Example 3

92 Faversham Street

Weybridge

Surrey

020 8 123 6789

Mr. J Baldrick

Baldrick Enterprises

Jones Street

Northampton

N1 4RG

5th October any date

Dear Mr Baldrick

Please find enclosed my application form for the post of computer manager advertised recently in the Times Newspaper.

I look forward to hearing from you soon.

Yours sincerely

Rupert James

Letters to agencies/consultants

Again, when writing to agencies and consultants, employ exactly the same rules of letter writing but be more specific about what you want if you are writing general letters, not in response to a specific advertisement.

You may wish to give the consultant more information so that he/she can suggest vacancies that you may be interested in applying for. You need to convince the consultant that you are proficient in your chosen field. Therefore, your application must look professional. Remember that it will go from the consultant to a number of companies.

The golden rule throughout letter writing is that a letter must be laid out on quality paper, well written, clear and to the point.

Now read the key points from chapter nine overleaf.

**

KEY POINTS FROM CHAPTER NINE
COVERING LETTERS

■ Always send a covering letter with a CV or application form

■ Always use good quality paper

■ Always type your letter if your handwriting is not so good

■ Letters must always be formal, never familiar

■ Spend some time laying out the letter

■ Be brief and clear-short and too the point!

**

Section 5

Application Forms

Ch: 10

Application Forms

If you are applying for a job that requires you to fill in an application form, there are several important rules to remember. When you receive the form never fill in the original in the first instance. You might make a mistake and not be happy with what you have written and might need to start again. By then, if you are using the original, it will be too late. Always copy the form and fill it in with a pencil. This way, you will not suffer if you make a mistake.

Application forms can either be written or word processed. It is up to you to exercise your discretion at this point. However, only if your handwriting is neat should you fill in the form by hand. A word processed form will be more immediately readable and make a better first impression. many applications forms can be completed on-line so this should not be a problem.

Send the application form in with a brief covering letter. Do not falsify the application form, as this will form part of your contract of employment when offered the post.

The job application should be treated much the same way as your CV. As we discussed, when you interpret the job advertisement you need to analyze the nature of the job before compiling the CV. You should do exactly the same with an application form. The first task is to read the job description that should normally accompany the application form.

It is absolutely essential that you understand the requirements of the post. Many organizations will send a person specification that outlines the essential and desirable criteria, which the applicant must meet before he or she is considered for the post. Although the essential criteria are the most important, if those short listing for the post have a number of good candidates then they will revert to the desirable criteria as a way of further eliminating candidates.

It follows that, when completing an application form, which has a person specification in it, then you should fill in the application carefully following the requirements of the post, ensuring that you meet the essential and desirable criteria. In addition to essential and desirable criteria, there will be a skills required section, which will generally outline the skills and abilities, which the person must demonstrate.

Make sure that when you fill in your application form that you follow the person specification closely, you have read and understood the job description and that you comply with all the requirements. If you do not, then you are wasting your time. Normally, there is a space on an application form, which asks you to outline your experience to

88

date and to demonstrate why you want the job. You should be concise and to the point. On too many application forms, applicants really go to town in this section, producing a whole life history amounting to many sides of paper. This is totally unnecessary and will, more often that not, result in your application being thrown in the bin.

You should follow carefully the requirements of the post, from the person specification to the job description, and lay out clearly and concisely your experience to date. You should then relate this to the job on offer and explain why you think that you are the ideal candidate. If there is no job description or person specification to work from, then you will need to read very carefully the requirements of the post from the advertisement, and then construct what you think are the main aspects of the job related to your own experience.

In this way, you can present the interviewer with a picture of yourself. It is not very often these days that an application form is not accompanied by a job description.

If you feel that you are on uncertain ground, for example when faced with filling in an application form without a job description or person specification, then you might want to contact the company concerned and request further information.

Content of application forms

The application form will proceed on a logical progressive basis, much as a CV is compiled. The form will start by asking you your name and address, some will ask your date of birth. The type of organization that you are applying to will very much determine the application you are being asked to fill in.

Some application forms are designed with great care and reflect the ethos of the organization, such as omitting to ask certain information on an equal opportunities ground. For example, some organizations deliberately do not ask for information relating to age as this is thought to affect the perceptions of those who are short listing for the post.

There will be a space for a phone number. This is important, as the company may want to contact you by phone shortly after the interview to discuss the possibilities of offering you a job.

Other details at the beginning of an application form might be sex, marital status and country and place of birth. This again will vary depending on the organization you are applying to. The next section of the form will ask you for details of education. You should start with your most recent job first. However, it is very important to read the application form as it might state otherwise.

Applications might ask for salary information and reasons for leaving the post. As discussed, on a CV it is not wise to volunteer this information, with the exception of final salary. However, some application forms may require this and will say so.

90

If the state of your health has not involved disability but has involved long periods off work then you should try to demonstrate to your employer that this problem is now in the past and that this will not affect your future employment.

Most applications end by asking for references. These will normally be from your current employer and one other, such as someone who has known you for a long time. If you are not currently employed then the reference should be from your ex-employer. Make sure that you know what your employer or ex- employer is going to say about you in advance. It follows that you should let this person know that you are going to use them as a reference.

Many employers do not bother taking up references despite asking for them. Others always take them up as a matter of course. Some applications state that they will take up references when a candidate is short-listed. You should contact the company and state that you do not want this as it could affect your relationship with your employer (if this is the case).

If you have not yet been employed then you should use school or academic references. A second reference might be a personal reference. Some applications will ask specifically for a personal reference. In this case, it is better to use a professional reference, i.e. someone with whom you have worked in a voluntary capacity or even someone you have worked in a paid capacity for.

There are a number of other questions that may appear on an application form, such as whether or not you have a driving license or whether you speak any other languages. Notice periods, possible start dates and periods of notice, plus membership of professional bodies may also appear.

There may also be a requirement to outline your ambitions. Be careful and tailor this to your employer's requirements.

Now read the key points from chapter ten overleaf.

**

KEY POINTS FROM CHAPTER TEN

APPLICATION FORMS

■ Always fill in a copy of the original application form. Use a pencil to do this. Only when you are happy with the original product should you transfer it to the original.

■ You should always type the form unless your handwriting is very neat.

■ Send the form with a brief covering letter.

■ Read the job description and person specification carefully. Fill the form in following the requirements of the post.

■ Be concise and keep to the point, particularly in the experience to date section of the form.

■ If there is no job description and person specification, and you are in doubt, then you should contact the company concerned and request more details.

■ Check with potential referees before using them.

Section 6

Other tips

Ch: 11

Most Common C.V. Writing Mistakes

When putting together your C.V. there are certain things that you need to watch out for. Would be employers spot these things and they can make a difference. Remember, first impressions are lasting impressions!

CV's and photographs of yourself

In the main, unless you are applying for a position as an actor or actress, photographs should not be included on a CV. The recruiter is only interested in brief, factual information.

Take care with headings

The first thing to appear on your CV should be your name. You don't need to head with 'Curriculum Vitae' This is outdated and could, in any case, lead to embarrassing typos, as it is easy to misspell Curriculum Vitae.

Get your email address right

You should ensure that you have written your email address correctly. This is a common mistake and can be costly. Also, make sure that it is there in the first place!

Section headings

Make sure that the section headings are clear and logical. It is very important that the recruiter can scan the CV quickly and with minimum effort. This book has been about the information that should be in a CV, make sure that it is well laid out. make sure that you use bullet points as and where appropriate.

Excessive details

Ensure that you keep you CV lean and mean, don't describe too much, particularly in the area of personal interest. The CV is the way in to the interview and should not be over the top.

Information concerning referees

Whether you include details of referees or not very much depends on the circumstances of each job. Generally, don't include them unless needed at that stage. Just a simple statement 'references are available on request will do.

Length of CV

Your CV should be no longer than 2 pages. One will do when necessary. Many people seem to think that a CV should be akin to an autobiography, another common mistake. Once again, keep it lean and mean.

**

Ch:12

Professions where the rules for writing CV's are different

Although the rules of CV writing relate to all types of professions, it is the case that there will be particular requirements for specialized roles. the following job specialisms will require a slightly different CV:

Medical CV's

Here you will need to demonstrate ongoing educational attainments and also:

- Clinical skills
- Audits
- Research
- Presentations
- Publications
- Teaching experience

You will usually include full details of your references/referees and also details of your professional registrations and status.

Two good sites for gleaning further information about producing a medical CV are www.medicalinterviewsuk.co.uk also www.bma.org.uk/advice/career/applying-for-a-job/medical-cv

Academic and scientific CV's

Academic CV's are very similar to medical CV's in that you need to include more detail about your professional accomplishments and also publications. The key extra features compared to general CVs are more focus on: publications your research activities funding awarded. Although academic CVs are longer than other types of CVs, no more than four pages is usual.

A useful website which will help in compiling an academic CV is www.vitae.ac.uk/researcher-careers/pursuing-an-academic-career/how-to-write-an-academic-cv. Also www.elsevier.com/connect/writing-an-effective-academic-cv.

Teaching CV's

Teaching CV's will require more information concerning your teaching career and the level you have reached to date. CPD (Continuing Professional Development) is important and will need to be clearly shown on your CV. IT skills will need to be highlighted as they are becoming increasingly important especially with interactive learning resources now being commonplace.

Extra-curricular activities are important within a teaching context. Recruiters will be looking for evidence that you really want to get involved in all aspects of school life, contribute to the community and build relationships with your students both in and out of the classroom.

A good website which offers advice and also CV templates for teachers is www.teacherstalk.co.uk/resources/teaching_cv.php

Legal CV's

Although legal CV's are very similar to ordinary CV's there are a couple of major differences that you need to be aware of.

The fact that the legal sector is very competitive indeed means that prospective employers will concentrate on your academic background in greater detail. As such, a legal CV should be very comprehensive in this respect, including full details of institutions attended and also grades received. Any accomplishments in court should be briefly included.

A useful website detailing legal CV layouts is www.allaboutlaw.co.uk/law-careers/law-cv/law-cv-template.

IT CV's

IT CV's are almost always very complex and it is vital to focus on communicating extensive information clearly and concisely. be very careful in the use of jargon.

You should take a very functional approach with this type of CV, highlighting your specific technical skills, broken down into categories, such as:

- Hardware
- Software
- Programming languages
- Network protocols

You should also flag up any relevant affiliations, such as memberships of any societies and professional bodies. Again, an IT CV can run on for three or four pages. A useful website for IT sample CV's is www.cvtemplatemaster.com/cv-template/developer-free-cv-template-in-ms-word.

Other useful websites are:

Engineering CV's

www.dayjob.com/engineering-cv-template-268

Architecture and Design CV's

www.archdaily.com/793375/the-top-architecture-resume-cv-designs

Performing arts CV's

www.livecareer.co.uk/cv-search/performing-arts

Military/Civilian transition CV's

This is a very big change, the transition from military to civilian life and it is important to show just what experience you have and how this can be translated into civilian life. help is always provided by the military but there are also a few useful websites that can help with CV writing:

www.cvspecialist.org.uk/militarytocivilianlifecv.

www.ctp.org.uk/resettlement-guides/cv+writing

**

Ch:13

Producing a CV When Looking for Work Abroad- General Tips

Creating a More Global CV

For starters, every CV you submit should be tailored for the specific job to which you are applying, and, of course, it will have to be tailored to the specific countries and cultural environments where you are seeking employment. There is no way to come up with just one CV that works for every job sector in every country on Earth.

Create a Master List of Your Experiences for Reference

The goal of the CV, in the U.S., Europe, Asia, or anywhere, is to help you stand out from the crowd and ultimately land an interview. It is NOT a complete synopsis of everything you've ever done. In fact, you should only list experiences directly relevant to the position you are applying for.

A master list of your experiences is for your reference only, so whenever you apply for a new job, you can pick and choose experiences from the master template and easily customize your CV.

This could be especially helpful, for example, if you have experience in finance, sales, and international development, and want to apply for jobs in each of these very distinct fields. If you apply for a business development role in an international aid organization, you may want to include some relevant sales experience. If you apply for a finance role in a global multinational, you may also want to include some, but not all, of your international development experience.

How Many Pages Should it Be?

As we have seen, In the UK job market, the general rule is to keep your CV to a single page although this depends on the sector. Everywhere else in the world has a much more flexible standard, usually 2-4 pages, with the longer side accommodating truly seasoned professionals.

What About a Photo?

There is no set rule about this, but, unlike the UK, it is common in Europe and Asia to include a professional portrait when submitting a CV. For other jobs, especially client-facing ones, the human resources rep sifting through piles of resumes may favour one that includes a photo of a well-dressed, attractive-looking candidate.

However, we also live in a very digital and visual age, and any recruitment professional will take a lap around Google gathering information about a prospective candidate, so they will probably see photos of you anyway. Many experts actually think that adding a well-selected photo to your resume can add an element of personality, openness, and confidence to your application that positively sets you apart.

What About Fonts, Colours, and Design?

As we have emphasised, the basic principle of CV design is universal: keep it simple, clean, and easy to read. Your CV should be black and white with a minimum size 10 sans-serif font. Use standard one inch margins.

If you feel the need to adjust your margins to accommodate more content, you need to either streamline what you are including or move everything onto an additional page. There should be no half pages of content, so only include an additional page if you can fill it meaningfully. Otherwise, cut back and stick to fewer pages.

How Much Personal Information Should I Include?

Many Europeans and Asians will include their nationality, gender, date of birth, and marital status on their CV's. If you're applying for a job in an unfamiliar country, you might want to ask a local friend (or friend of friend) to see a sample CV. One of the most important aspects when applying for a job overseas, in a Non-English speaking country, is that you speak the language of that country. This should be clearly indicated, along with any other languages that you speak.

To be safe-stick to global best practices

More or less this would be:

- 2 pages
- Current contact details
- An enhanced personal data profile
- Education details and qualifications from both secondary school and institutions of higher education
- Concise bullet-points under each work experience detailing achievements and responsibilities
- A section that summarises technical skills and spoken languages (with a clear indication of your native language)
- A professional portrait photo at the top (depending on the job)

In any case, the hiring manager will see that you are coming from a different country and will take that into consideration when reviewing your CV. As long as you provide enough information to allow the representative to assess your abilities for the role, it's hard to go wrong.

In the End, You Have to Speak the Right Language. The most important thing of all, beyond the number of pages or whether or not you include a photo, is that you speak their language. Not as in German or Spanish, but the language of the job description and the company you are applying to.

Use key words from their website and the job solicitation on your CV in order to reflect their values and expertise back to them. Show them you've done your homework and have internalised the nature of the company to the degree that you, while showcasing all your true abilities, already look and sound like you work for them.

**

Ch: 14

Where and How to Send your CV

It is true to say that companies are always in the process of recruiting, even in these straitened times. Most companies, particularly the bigger ones will experience a fairly high turnover of staff per annum. Companies therefore have vacancies and it is imperative that your CV is available to view at the right moment.

There are a number of ways to distribute your CV other than the time-honored method of forwarding it direct to the employer when a vacancy is advertised. Below, we look at the most effective ways. In appendix one there are a number of Internet sites listed to which you can send your CV.

Distribution of your CV through the internet

There are two main forms of electronic CV distribution through the Internet:

- Posting your CV in CV banks, which are searched by corporate recruiters and also headhunters
- Sending your CV direct to an employers website.

CV banks

There are a lot of CV banks where your CV can be posted for free. A search online, merely tapping in the words CV bank will bring up sites. Most of these sites have standardized CV forms which you must fill in. Every time you post a CV online in this way it will be seen by a lot of potential employers. These banks are periodically cleaned out, every three months or so, so make a note of when a CV was posted.

Employers web sites

Posting your CV to individual employers web sites obviously takes longer than posting it to a CV bank but it is more direct and is guaranteed to reach your target. Most employers web sites have a recruitment section where the posting can take place. Again, company databases are purged at frequent intervals so it is up to you to monitor the situation.

Web CVs use HTML format. You can include the web address in an email or letter to an employer. They have the advantage that you can easily use graphics, colour, hyperlinks and even sound, animation and video. The basic rules still apply however - make it look professional. They can be very effective if you are going for multimedia, web design or computer games jobs where they can demonstrate your technical skills along with your portfolio.

LinkedIn

It's a good idea to have your profile and CV (without personal details such as your address of course: see right) on LinkedIn. In 2011, 89% of businesses planned to use social networks for recruitment and LinkedIn was by far the most popular one for this purpose with 86% of companies wishing to use it, 60% were considering Facebook and 50% Twitter. Make sure that your Facebook page doesn't carry evidence of any of your indiscretions that employers might view - making your page private and viewable only by friends and family is wise!

Newspapers

Many people still use this tried and tested route, mass mailing of CV's to many companies. It is advisable to check that you are buying the right target paper for your own desired area of employment. For example, the guardian has main days, usually Tuesday and Wednesday when it advertises a whole range of jobs, from media to education to housing to social work.

It is important to identify which day is appropriate for you and also to see in the adverts whether CV's are acceptable. Not all companies or prospective employers accept CV's.

Employment agencies

There are many agencies in the market place all competing for work. Many agencies are specialist, specializing in certain types of skillsets, i.e. construction, driving, social work, housing, secretarial and so on.

You should identify the list of agencies appropriate to you and send a copy of your updated CV to them. They will then contact you and, usually, ask you to come in for an interview. Many will ask if it is OK to take up references and some will take up a CRB (criminal records) check, depending on the type of work being undertaken.

Vocational and college placement offices

Obviously, if you are a student and have access to this resource then it is essential that you make use of it.

Business and trade publications

Many trades and businesses have their own publications and often will advertise jobs in these. The construction industry and social work plus housing sectors all have their own journals. A library is a good place to start with narrowing down specific journals.

The importance of following up

Having made a big effort in producing your CV and then having, one way or another, sent it to prospective employers, it is essential that
114

you follow up your efforts. If you don't do this then it is highly likely That your CV will sit in some busy person's in-tray for ages. A call to the appropriate person in human resources (personnel) will at least get you known to the company and may move you a few notches up the ladder.

**

Section 7

.

Interviews

Ch: 15

The Interview Stage and Pre-Interviews

In this chapter, we cover the more traditional face-to face interview. In Chapter 16, we cover remote interviews, such as through Skype and Zoom plus telephone interviews, which are becoming more prevalent now due to the pandemic and the increased incidence of home-working.

Having sent in your C.V or sent in your application form, at some point there will be a response, usually inviting you for an interview. Some firms will, on your arrival, ask you to sit a test. This should not usually be a surprise, as you will normally receive advance notice in the letter inviting you for an interview. It is advisable to know something about the nature of these tests before you arrive for the interview.

Therefore, before a more general discussion about interviews, it is necessary to discuss the range of tests that an employer may want you to carry out before or during the interview stage. The most common are known as psychological or psychometric tests.

Not all interviews are preceded by a test of this sort, but they are becoming common enough to warrant a discussion in order to give an idea of what may be faced.

A psychometric test is simply a standard way of measuring some specific attribute or aspect of mental behavior. It is standard because everyone who does a particular test is treated in exactly the same way, as are the results. The idea is to produce an objective summary of what a person is or is not good at and how they come across as an individual. There are literally thousands of different tests on the market, measuring a whole different range of attributes.

Most measure one or other of the following:

- Attainment. Your learnt ability, for example what you know about arithmetic or spelling
- Aptitude. Your ability to acquire further knowledge or skills for example your understanding of words or ideas
- Personality. What you are like as a person, for example, are you outgoing or quiet and thoughtful?
- Values. What you think is important, for example money or power, or both
- Interests. What would you like to do or what activities do you think would suit you best? For example, would you prefer to fell trees or write newspaper articles
- Skills. What you have learnt to do practically, for example there are standard tests for differing occupations.

Psychometric tests require you to answer all the questions and there is only one correct answer. You are not expected to finish in the time allowed, thereby distinguishing tests from exams.

Tests can measure lots of separate abilities of which the most common are:

- Verbal ability
- Numerical ability
- Perceptual ability (understanding and reasoning)
- Spatial ability. How well you picture shapes being moved in three dimensions
- Mechanical ability
- Abstract ability. How well you can analyze a problem.
- Clerical ability. How well you understand simple arithmetic and use of English.

All these tests can be used by themselves or in combination. There are also tests for people with different levels of ability, such as those specially designed for graduates or managers.

Personality tests

The ancient Greeks arrived at four basic personality tests and in the twentieth century, scientists have refined these as follows:

- Extrovert-introvert
- Confident-anxious
- Structured-non structured
- Conformist-non-conformist

Personality tests attempt to measure where you come on these scales.

Preparing for tests

Although your early life will prepare you for tests, there are certain things that you can do to improve your performance. You should ensure that:

- You have some information on your potential employer on the sort of thing that you will be doing.
- Have an understanding what testing is like, what the experience is like.

There are many books on the market ranging from personality to I.Q tests. It is worth investing in such a book, or visiting your local library and spend some time doing a few selected tests.

To ensure that everyone has an equal chance to do their best, most tests are administered under carefully controlled conditions. This means that you complete the tests sitting at a desk facing a test administrator. As many tests are given to groups, you will find yourself sitting in a row, schoolroom fashion with other candidates.

The test administrator will:

- Welcome you and introduce him/herself.
- Explain the purpose of the test.
- Detail the nature of the tests.
- Explain how the tests are to be administered.

Although most personality tests are un-timed, you are expected to finish in a reasonable time, about 35-45 minutes.

The test administrator will:
- Read out instructions for the test.
- Ask you to complete some practice questions and/or explain some worked examples.
- Tell you how much time you have for the test.
- Stop the test when appropriate and introduce the next one.
- Close the session and give you some information on what will happen next.

Assessment of tests

With ability tests, the employer will look to see how many questions have been answered correctly. This gives you what is known as the raw score. Your raw score is then standardized using something called a normative group. This is a large representative sample of people who have done the test in the past, including current jobholders, graduates, managers and the general population, among others.

When scores have been standardized they can be compared on an objective basis with other peoples, and employers can see if you have scored above or below average and also how much above or below. Personality tests operate in a slightly different way because there are no right or wrong answers. However, comparisons can be made within a normative group and allow employers to see, for example, if you are more or less extroverted that the average person.

Once standardized, test results can be used in one of two ways: as a source of information, which can be used at interview or as a screening device. When results are used to screen candidate's two further selection techniques can be used: top down or minimum cut off. Top down means that candidates are picked on the basis of highest scores leading down. Minimum cut off selects everyone who scores over a set level. Again, personality tests are different since it makes no sense to use top down or minimum cut off. However,

124

candidates may be selected out if they score at the wrong extreme on a critical dimension.

If you have been tested and have been unsuccessful at this stage then the employer will always usually be prepared to give you feedback on your tests. This can often be very useful. It is now time to discuss interviews generally. Not all employers will give you a test and, as stated, often tests are carried out prior to undertaking the interview.

The interview

You do not get to the interview stage unless the employer believes that you can do the job. This means that you have already been accepted on the basis of your C.V or application. You supply all the information about yourself. This means that while the interviewer controls the structure of the interview, decisions can only be made on the basis of what you provide.

Most of the interview questions can be predicted in advance. This being the case, you can prepare answers in your own time, which cast you in the most positive light.

Before we look at interview tactics, it is useful to know that there are a number of different types of interview. There are three main variations:

- Single. This is a one to one meeting between the interviewer and candidate. Of all the types of interview, it is the most relaxing for both interviewer and interviewee alike. This type of interview is favored by smaller organizations although there can be a potential for bias.
- Sequential interview. This is where there is a series of interviews, usually two or maybe three, carried out by different interviewers. It allows for a range of impressions to be gathered.

Although in theory this process should be more democratic, in practice the most senior interviewer will have the most sway

.

- Panel interview. This involves being questioned by a number of interviewers, in turn at the same interview. This type of interview is popular in most organizations and the number of interviewers varies. The type of person interviewing will vary depending on the type of organization.

The facts about interviews

The latest figures show that 90% of organizations use interviews. Interviewers will make up their mind quite rapidly, usually after the first four or five minutes. Making a positive first impression is very important indeed. Different interviewers set different standards. They pay attention to information that is out of the ordinary and are more influenced by negative information than positive.

Interviewers are not very good at assessing real personality. This is not really possible in such a short space of time. Characteristics often begin to manifest themselves several weeks into the job. How you are judged during and after an interview depends very much on whom the interviewer has seen. This is known technically as the Halo effect.

There are many other points about interviews, one main one being that subjectivity will creep in, i.e. how well your face fits, whether you are considered to be a team player and so on. At the end of the day you have to fit into the organization and those interviewing will only employ you if this is perceived to be the case.

Preparing for interviews

Although some of the negative aspects of the interview process have been stressed, you should always try to be positive. You need to pay a lot of attention to preparing for the interview. A few preliminary points need to be considered:

- Do you know exactly where and what time the interview is taking place. This may sound silly, but in your initial

127

excitement and haste, you may overlook it until the last moment and may find yourself at a disadvantage.

- Do you know who is going to be interviewing you, their name and job title?
- Do you know enough about the organization, have you researched them and do you know enough about their history and product?

Presentation

This is of the utmost importance. What you wear will have to be appropriate to the type of business you are dealing with. You are going to a business meeting so you should wear the smartest clothes that you can and dress conservatively. Dark colors shave a greater impact. The main point here is that you should not disadvantage yourself, no matter what your outlook on life. You may secretly hate wearing a suit and tie but in order to get the job you want you have to bend to the whims of the employer. Remember, they have the power in this situation and you have to prove yourself.

Materials

Don't forget to take your C.V or application to the interview. Also take a pen and paper for taking notes. Prepare some questions to ask the interviewers when the interview is over.

128

There is nothing worse than saying that you have no questions. This disappoints the interviewers and leads them to think that you are not very interested in their organization.

Making an Impression

As mentioned, research has shown that interviewers usually make up their minds during the first few minutes and spend the rest of the interview trying to confirm this impression. First impressions are based on several things: what you look like and how you behave. The impression that you make will, to a large degree, depend on the interviewer and his or her prejudices and dislikes and overall bias.

Body language

This bit will require some practice. Obviously, your body language will vary depending on the situation you are in, those in front of you and how you feel at the time. The impression that you will make will rest on:

- Facial expression and how you move your head.
- What you do with your hands and arms.
- What you do with the rest of your body.

It is also useful to know that, in terms of being believable, the most accurate signals someone gives out are such things as going pale, swallowing and sweating, which are automatic, followed by what you do with your legs and feet and the rest of your body. A few important points:

- Look at the interviewer and smile.
- Nod your head to show that you are paying attention.
- Lean forward when speaking and back when listening.

At the same time:

- Do not make sudden movements.
- Do not fold your arms.

In particular, sit in a relaxed manner and do not fidget. This means do not move about on the seat and keep your feet and hands still. You need to give the interviewer the impression of being business like and confident, genuinely interested in the position on offer.

The structure of the interview

At the outset, the interviewer will try to relax you and break the ice. An effort will be made to explain the interview process to you. There

130

is a fairly common format to the interview process and this will normally tie in to the C.V or application form.

The interviewer will begin by talking about the organization and its history and future plans. Then you will be invited to tell the interviewer(s) about your own recent work history and how it fits in with the job on offer. They may even ask you at this stage why you have applied for the post although this normally comes later. Generally, the questions related to the post will begin at this time. The interviewers will ask you structured questions. Usually, candidates for a job will get asked the same questions. This, however, will vary depending on the post, the organization and other factors.

At the end of the questions you will normally be told about the terms and conditions, and also about the interview process, i.e. when they expect to be able to make a decision.

There are many variations on the above theme. During the course of the interview, the person(s) interviewing may decide to concentrate more on you and ask you about your aspirations. You should always be cautious here and appear ambitious but not unrealistic. If your employer thinks that they cannot meet your aspirations then it may cost you your job. They may try to gauge your interests and your circumstances in order to build up a clearer picture of you and try to get a picture of your background.

This very much depends on the job and interviewers. It is the practice in the public sector, for example, to try to remain as objective as possible, also in larger private sector organizations. However, this may differ radically in other organizations depending on size, nature of the operation and so on.

There are a few golden rules in interviews. Never get too aggressive or arrogant in front of the interviewers. This can happen for a number of reasons. It can be down to nervousness, insecurity or the fact that you are doing badly, or at least you feel you are and try to mask this by being hostile or aggressive.

If you fall into this mode of behavior then you will almost certainly not get the job. If you feel that you cannot answer a question then you should ask the person to go back to it later. This will give you more time to focus your mind and relax.

Earlier, we talked about preparation. Part of preparation is mental preparation. Putting you into the right frame of mind and becoming confident.

If you stop to think about it, all you are doing is sitting in front of people who work for a firm, who wish you no harm and want to see you succeed. If you think yourself into this frame of mind, then even if you get the idea that you are not doing well then you can still retain your self-confidence and dignity.

How do interviewers make decisions?

A good interviewer will assess you against the requirements for the job. This means that your particular skills, abilities, experiences and knowledge will be matched against a list of essential and desirable qualities. It might be that a particular sort of business experience is required and ideally the employer is seeking certain types of qualifications. The list is known as the person specification, and the better the fit between you and the person specification the greater the chances of getting the job.

This makes it sound simple, in reality however the process is quite complicated. The reason for this is that certain sorts of information appear to be more influential than others. The following factors are seen to be particularly influential:

- Personality. How you present yourself as a person.
- Experience. The experience you have that is relevant to the job.
- Qualifications. The qualifications that you have which are relevant to the job.
- Background. Your general work background and your track record.
- Enthusiasm. How motivated and interested you appear to be about the job.
- Education. Your general level of educational experience.

133

This list reinforces the critical need to make a powerful and positive impression on the employer. It also stresses the need to relate experience, qualifications and general work background to the job in question and give the impression that you are an energetic and motivated individual with a genuine interest in the work and the employer's organization. Whatever the method of assessing the information or the weight given to it, the end result is that you will eventually be offered a job or turned down. This process takes time and during this period another part of the selection system comes into operation. The employer will offer the job to the best candidate but the second or even the third will not be rejected. Someone is always kept in reserve in case the first candidate rejects the job offer.

In general, if you have not heard anything after ten days, contact the employer and ask if a decision has been made. Sometimes, people are actually offered a job at the interview. If this happens to you, remember that it could mean a number of things:

- The employer is very impressed.
- You have undersold yourself.
- The employer is desperate

In relation to underselling yourself, you should leave all salary negotiations to the end of the selection process. If you are asked what you expect to be paid, give a range and ask what the rate for the job is.

134

The point is that you are in a much more powerful negotiating position when someone actually wants you and genuinely believes that you are the best person for the job.

Reading the signs

Before the final decision, you can get some indication of your performance if you consider what happened at the interview. Positive signs include:

- Any detailed discussions about salary.
- Any exploration of when you can start the job.
- An interview that lasts longer than expected.
- An interview, which includes unscheduled meetings with other decision makers, such as managers.
- Being invited to a second interview.

In contrast, negative signs are:

- An interview, which is much shorter than anticipated, perhaps only 20 minutes long.
- Being repeatedly caught out by the interviewer and not being able to answer the questions.
- An obvious clash between your personal requirements and what the company can provide, for example in terms of work hours.

135

After the interview, if you have been turned down, you should contact the company and try to get feedback from the interview. This can be invaluable and put you on the right track for the next interview.

Now read the Key points from Chapter Fifteen overleaf.

**

KEY POINTS FROM CHAPTER FIFTEEN

THE INTERVIEW STAGE AND PRE-INTERVIEW TESTS

■ It is advisable to know something about pre-interview/interview tests before the interview stage.

■ The most common tests are psychological and psychometric tests.

■ Psychometric tests measure lots of abilities, most commonly verbal, numerical, perceptual, spatial, mechanical, abstract and clerical abilities.

■ Personality tests measure the nature of your personality, i.e., extrovert, introvert, confidence etc.

■ Most interview questions can be predicted in advance. You should prepare thoroughly by rehearsing possible questions.

■ Always present the best side of yourself and be as relaxed as possible.

■ Always be prepared and take your C.V or application form.

Chapter 16

How to Perform Well in Remote Interviews

What are Remote Interviews?

They are real interviews held over the phone or by methods such as Zoom/Skype or by video, rather than face-to-face. Remote interviews have been much more common during the pandemic. You will usually be interviewed by a member of the graduate recruitment or HR team. In normal times, a telephone interview will usually be given to candidates who have passed the online application and/or psychometric test stage of the graduate recruitment process and is used to sift out applicants to be invited to a face-to-face interview or assessment centre. May of the principles applying to Skype also apply to Zoom.

Who uses telephone interviews?

You are more likely to have a telephone interview with one of the large corporate recruiters than with a small or medium sized company. Telephone interviews are used by all kinds of employers – banks, accountancy and law firms, consultancies, retailers, manufacturing companies etc. Companies that use telephone interviews include Tesco, HSBC, Corus, BT, Lloyds of London, Shell, GlaxoSmithKline, Vodaphone, BSkyB and many others.

They are especially common for sales-related jobs, such as recruitment consultancy and particularly (surprise!) telesales, where verbal communication skills are paramount. You may also expect a telephone interview if you are applying for jobs abroad – in which case calls may come in at all hours of the day or night!

How long do they last?

Based on a small sample of people who have had telephone interviews, they varied in length from 20 minutes to 1 hour, with the average length being half an hour:

Advantages of telephone interviews

For the employer:

They are time and cost-effective - most last about 20-25 minutes.

They test your verbal communication skills and telephone technique.

For you:

You can refer (quickly!) to your application form, take notes – even hold on to your teddy bear for moral support. You don't need to dress up or smarten up. However, you might feel that you want to do this to give yourself moral support.

140

You don't need to spend time travelling to interview or wonder if the employer will pay your expenses.

Disadvantages of telephone interviews (for you)

You can't see the interviewer to gauge their response.

Tension – you never know when an employer might call to interview you.

They can seem to go very quickly, without giving you much time to think about your answers - so be well prepared!

The advertisement may ask you to phone the company.

This gives you total control over the time and place of the interview – although means that you will have to pay for the call. At the time arranged, make sure you are in a quiet location and that you will not be disturbed during the call. Or they may phone you in response to your CV/application form

You will normally be advised when the telephone call will be made so always be prepared for this:

Keep your mobile with you, charged, topped up and switched on at the appropriate time! Make sure that the reception is OK. Try and take the phone to as quiet and private a location as possible.

If the call does come unexpectedly and you are not prepared say *"Thank you for calling, do you mind waiting for a minute while I close*

141

the door/turn off the radio/take the phone to a quieter room?". This will give you a little time to compose yourself.

If it really is a bad time, offer to call back, fix a time and stick to it. Check your answerphone message: is it one that you would want a prospective employer to hear? Does it give a professional impression? If not, change it – just in case you do miss a call for any reason.

Tips

Keep a copy of your application and information on the company handy, plus a pen and notepad to take notes. Have your laptop turned on if your application is on this.

Before the call, make a list of your USP's (unique selling points): the things that make you better in some ways than most of the other people who will be applying.

Don't just read out your notes as this will sound stilted. It's useful to have a glass of water to hand during a phone interview (but move the phone away from your mouth when you swallow). You will be doing a lot of talking and you don't want your mouth to dry up at a crucial moment!

Smile when you dial! (and, more importantly, when you speak): it really does make a difference to your tone of voice. Although the interviewer can't see you, you may find it easier to come over in a "professional" manner if you are sitting at a desk or table rather than lounging in bed.

In a face to face interview, you show that you are listening via non-verbal signals such as nodding your head. Over the phone you have to show this by the occasional *"OK"*, *"uh-huh"*, *"I see"*, *"I understand"*, *"yes"* or similar interjections. Listen very carefully to the interviewer and try to answer with a lively tone of voice. Speak clearly and not too fast. Reflect back what the speaker is saying in other words. This shows you're listening carefully and checks you are understanding. It is often the most useful way of giving positive feedback to someone: "I hear what you're saying and take it seriously". You can't keep saying "uh-huh" or "yes" for too long without it sounding false. Immediately after the interview, write down the questions you were asked and any ways in which you could have improved your responses.

What questions will I be asked?

These will be identical to those asked in a face-to-face interview!

Will I be given any tests?

Perhaps – tests can quite easily be administered over the phone. The interviewer may read out a series of statements and you will be asked to say if you agree or disagree. Sometimes this can be done by pressing the telephone keys. The tests involved are more likely to be personality-type questions than reasoning tests. For example, you may be asked to rate the extent to which you felt the following activities reflect your personal style, from 1 (not at all) to 5 (a lot):

Meeting new people

Setting yourself targets to achieve

Working on your own

Repairing mechanical equipment

Video/Zoom interviews

As technology continues to grow, and as virtual work becomes more accepted, Skype interviews become closer to the norm for many industries and roles. A Skype interview requires just as much, if not more, preparation than you'd take on for an in-person interview. Preparation can ensure that you can combat technical issues, know how to appear well on camera and have a successful Skype Interview.

What is Skype

Skype is a video conferencing program that allows for remote interviews over your computer or phone rather than appearing in-person. You should treat an interview on Skype similarly to one that would normally be face-to-face. Below are tips for a Skype job interview:

Make sure you have Skype installed.

Dress professionally.

Use an appropriate background

Face the light.

Sit at a proper distance.

Arrange the Skype windows.

Test your microphone and video.

Take the interview in a quiet location.

Log in a little early.

Show engagement in the conversation.

Take turns speaking.

Prepare for the interview.

Maintain good posture.

Share your screen.

Record your interview.

Make sure you have Skype installed

If you don't use Skype regularly, make sure you have the program installed on your computer ahead of time. Downloading and going through the installation process can take a long time, so you don't want to do this right before your interview and risk showing up late. If you already have Skype installed, make sure it's updated and you have your log-in credentials handy so you don't have to reset your password beforehand.

Dress professionally

Even though you aren't meeting in-person, you should still dress as if you are. That means appropriate business attire from head to toe, even if the interviewer won't be able to see all of your clothing. Look at how your outfit appears on camera, then consider your background and if your outfit of choice contrasts well. Staying in formal attire for a Skype interview will send the message you're very interested in and serious about the role.

Use an appropriate background

You can choose different backgrounds on Skype, which may be fun for a call with friends, but your best option for an interview is to either blur your background or make sure that what is behind you on video is appropriate. If you're taking the call in your bedroom, make sure your background is free of piles of laundry or an unmade bed. If your office tends to be a catch-all room, organize it before your interview so the only thing your interviewer is seeing behind you is a space that's well put together.

146

You can play it safe by setting up your desk in front of a solid, clean wall that's free of distractions.

Face the light

You'll want to be well lit during your interview so your potential new employer can see your facial expressions, engage with you and ensure the call goes smoothly. If you can, set up your computer so you're facing a window that lets in natural light or a desk lamp that will keep your face illuminated. No matter how it's done, it's important for the light source to appear behind your computer and focused on you.

When practicing your interview, take a look at how you appear in your outfit, background and light source of choice to make sure there isn't a distracting glare coming from any part of your setup.

Sit at a proper distance

During an in-person interview, you wouldn't sit on the opposite side of the room from the hiring manager. You also wouldn't sit uncomfortably close to them. Apply this same rule when on a Skype interview and maintain a proper distance between yourself and your computer camera.

When you test your video before entering the call, make sure that your face, shoulders and upper chest are visible, and that there is space between the top of your head and both sides of Your body in the shot. The more centered you are in the frame, the better your distance is.

Arrange the Skype windows

To make sure you're maintaining eye contact, arrange the video windows within the Skype program appropriately. When you open the software, the window with your hiring manager's video may be off to the side, so drag it over to be as close to the camera as possible. That way, your interviewer is seeing you look right at them and not anywhere else.

Test your microphone and video

Before your interview, test your microphone and video settings to make sure they work. If you go into the interview with working equipment, you're more likely to send the message that you have adequately prepared yourself for this meeting.

Your microphone should transmit your sound static-free and your speakers should work to receive audio from the hiring manager, while your video should be centered and camera clean.

To make sure everything is working as it should, visit your Skype settings and perform a test run of your equipment.

*

Take the interview in a quiet location

The amount of background noise during your interview can affect how well the call goes, so try to set up your computer in a space with the least amount of potential interruptions. Let those you live with know that you'll be taking an important call and that they shouldn't disturb you if they can help it. If there's a chance that an interruption will occur, such as with kids or dogs, be upfront with the hiring manager right away so they aren't too surprised if it happens. Consider silencing your phone and pausing pop-up notifications on your computer too.

Especially if your new job will require that you take customer or client calls or be a part of a lot of business meetings, your hiring manager may expect that you'll have a space dedicated to performing your work that will allow you to do so professionally. However, if an interruption happens during your interview, acknowledge it while remaining calm and focused on your discussion.

Log in a little early-Just as you arrive at an in-person interview a couple of minutes early, you should also try to arrive to the Skype interview early.

Depending on the Skype settings, you'll either be able to enter the meeting room before the interviewer, in which case they'll see you waiting once they've arrived, or you'll only be able to enter once the host has given you permission. In either case, a hiring Manager will

149

see that you are eager to chat about the role and adequately prepared for the interview.

Show engagement in the conversation

It's common for a hiring manager to rely heavily on body language as an accompaniment to what a potential hire is saying, but Skype interviews aren't exactly the same. Therefore, it's important to work at maintaining an engaging conversation through this platform. This means asking questions, nodding, keeping eye contact, smiling and acknowledging what the other person says.

Take turns speaking

While it's a great tip to remain conversational over video, you still must exercise some caution to make sure both parties hear each other and you both do not accidentally interrupt what the other is saying. Even unintentionally interrupting, like to answer the interviewer's question, can momentarily mute one person's microphone so the other can speak, a feature that can ultimately cause confusion and the need to repeat part of the conversation.

Prepare for the interview

As with any interview, prepare for the role by practicing your answers to popular interview questions, readying your portfolio, making notes of valuable responsibilities or projects that will showcase your experience and looking into the company you're applying with and the role you're interviewing for. You can also have some questions of your own prepared which shows that you put in the extra effort. Another way to prepare for the interview is by performing a test run with a friend on Skype. This will allow you to test your equipment and get used to speaking to someone over video. You may also want to read up on how to fix any technical issues and have that information in front of you before starting your interview. If your audio or video goes out or another common error occurs, you'll be better prepared to fix it quickly and get right back into the discussion.

Maintain good posture

Good posture showcases your professionalism, especially in this kind of scenario. While taking a seat in your favorite chair can entice you to slouch, be mindful of the posture you're using during the interview. Instead of sliding down in the chair, sit up straight with shoulders back and eyes forward. You may even communicate better and display more confidence with proper posture.

Share your screen

A significant benefit of a Skype interview is you can showcase your prior work as it relates to the role in a way that an in-person

151

interview may not afford. If you have an online portfolio, ask the hiring manager if you can share your screen so they can see your website, the social media accounts you've managed or sales numbers you have in a spreadsheet. Be prepared with this information in another window so you don't have to spend valuable time searching for it—this will also show that you prepared well for the interview.

Record your interview

Ask for permission to record the interview. Being able to refer back to the interview can help if you expect to have multiple Skype interviews before landing the role. You'll be able to both see how you can improve next time and prepare for the next steps based on information that you and the interviewer discussed.

Zoom interviews

Zoom is one of the medium used to carry out remote interviews. By now, you've probably heard of Zoom, the video-conferencing software has exploded in popularity since the start of the COVID-19 pandemic. People around the world are using it to stay connected with loved ones, host happy hours with friends, and, yes, even interview for jobs. If you have a job interview coming up on Zoom, you might feel intimidated — especially if you're not very familiar with the platform. Many of the tips relating to Skype are also pertinent to Zoom.

What is Zoom?

Zoom is an online platform for video and audio-conferencing, much like Skype, Google or even FaceTime. However, Zoom offers a lot more features, and many companies use it to host online meetings, training sessions, seminars, and now video interviews.

How to get started with Zoom

If you've never used Zoom, getting started is simple:

- Install Zoom on your computer. This takes less than a minute, but you'll want to do this with plenty of time before your interview, just in case something goes wrong.

- Open Zoom (this should happen automatically after you've installed it), and click "Join Meeting." There's no need to create an account unless you want to.

- Enter the meeting ID or personal link name, which the company you're interviewing with will provide. It'll likely be an 11-digit number. The company may also send a link over via email, which will bring you directly to the meeting.

- It's best to practice this a few times before your interview, just so you feel comfortable. It won't hurt to ask a friend or family member to hop in a Zoom meeting with you so you can test everything out.

On the day of your interview, join the meeting a couple of minutes before it officially begins. If the meeting host has not yet started the meeting, don't fret. As soon as the host joins, you'll be able to enter the meeting.

Preparing for your Zoom video interview

It's important to prepare for your video interview. In many ways, this will be easier than an in-person interview: You don't have to worry about traffic, and, if you're already employed, you won't have to worry about missing a huge amount of work. But there are still things to keep in mind.

Dress to impress

As we have stressed numerous times in this book, just like an in-person interview, carefully plan what you wear. Wear something polished and professional, but don't fret as much about what you wear from the chest down — you'll be on a video after all.

Location is key

You'll also need to scout out the perfect interviewing location in your home. Because we're all social distancing until the end of lockdown, companies will be more understanding and forgiving if you're interrupted by a partner, roommate, child, or pet; this situation is obviously not the norm.

Have a tech backup plan

Since you're relying on technology — which can be problematic just when you need it most — have your computer plugged in and charging. You'll also need a back-up plan, in case you have issues with your Wi-Fi internet connection. If you have an unlimited plan on your phone, you can connect your computer to its hotspot. Or you can download the Zoom app on your phone and have the meeting there. While this isn't ideal, it should work.

Make sure you can be seen and heard — and emote

Just like you would for an in-person interview, it's necessary to practice and prepare questions you want to ask — but there are a couple of additional things to keep in mind. First, make sure your audio works and your video camera is clear. If it's not, check out your Zoom settings by clicking the arrow next to "Stop Video." You'll find the audio settings there and can adjust accordingly.

Second, make sure your excitement and personality shows through the computer. This can be more difficult than it would be with an in-person interview, so focus on your body language, eye contact, tone and energy while you practice. If you want feedback, you can always

155

record yourself and watch it over, or connect with a professional interview coach, who will set up a mock video interview and provide feedback.

A few simple Zoom interview tips

Zoom has a lot of features, but you won't need to know all of them for your job interview. Instead, focus on these simple hacks to ensure your interview goes as smoothly as possible:

1. Use the video preview to your advantage

The nice thing about Zoom is it doesn't throw you into the video conference when you first join. Instead, it will show you a video preview. Use this as an opportunity to make sure your camera is smudge-free and perfectly positioned.

2. Touch yourself up

Not many people *love* staring at themselves in a camera, but Zoom has a feature that'll make you feel a little bit more polished. When you're in the video, click the arrow next to "Start Video" and go to settings. There, under the video tab, check the box that reads "Touch up my appearance." This adds a subtle filter to your screen that smooths out your appearance, toning down any splotches or blemishes you might be worried about.

156

3. Resist adding a virtual background

By now, you've probably seen all the creative backgrounds people have added to their Zoom meetings — from the set of "The Office" to Disney World to even outer space. Zoom basically turns your background into a green screen and lays an image over it.

Although you might be tempted, it's best to not use this feature during a video interviews. You'll want to stay as professional as possible, and the focus should be on you and the interviewer — not whatever's in the background. If your background is incredibly cluttered and you have no other option, look for a simple Zoom background, like a classic bookcase or a tidy office.

If you plan to use this feature, make sure you create a Zoom account and enable the virtual background set-up on your profile. Practice with it so you know it'll look good.

4. Utilize full-screen mode

Eliminate any potential distractions on your computer by closing any other tabs and making your Zoom window full screen with the "maximize" button on the top right side of your screen.

This is a super simple move, but it'll help you stay focused throughout your interview.

5. Choose your favourite layout

There are a few options for how you view your screen when using Zoom. Determine which layout you prefer from the following:

Active speaker: This will enlarge the video window of the person who is talking. So, if the interviewer is speaking, their video will take up the majority of your screen. If a second attendee is also on the video, then their screen will stay smaller until they begin speaking.

Gallery view: If you want everyone to be the same size, including yourself, choose gallery view. This will show all the meeting participants in a grid view. This makes it easy to view everyone at the same time.

To change your layout, select the option you want in the top right corner of your screen.

6. Know where your "mute" button is — just in case

In case of an emergency, you will want to know that your "mute" button is located in the bottom left corner of your Zoom window. Because you're interviewing at home, keep the mute button handy just in case the dog starts barking, the kids start screaming, or the fire alarm starts ringing.

The mute button is also a great way to help eliminate any background noise on your end while the interviewer is talking, especially if you live in a big city or on a busy street where sirens are commonplace.

Of course, in an ideal world, your Zoom job interviews will go flawlessly and be distraction free, but while everyone is at home during COVID-19, there are no guarantees. Just make sure you know how to properly use Zoom and do your best — Interviewers understand this is an unusual time for everyone.

Now read the key points from Chapter Sixteen overleaf.

****

KEY POINTS FROM CHAPTER 16

HOW TO PERFORM WELL IN REMOTE INTERVIEWS

- Phone interviews are real interviews held over the phone rather than face-to-face.

- You are more likely to have a phone interview with one of the larger corporate interviewers than with a smaller company.

- Following the pandemic, Skype/Zoom interviews are becoming more widely used, and are particularly useful for international interviews, such as for TEFL jobs

- A Skype/Zoom interview will be more like a real life interview than a telephone interview.

- The use of recorded video interviews is increasing. These started with technology companies, but have now spread to mainstream employers.

Final Comments

As you have seen, throughout this book the emphasis has been on care and quality, beginning with the interpretation of the job advert through to compiling your C.V and attending the interview.

The most important elements are:

- Be professional-take care with your presentation
- Believe in yourself
- Do not be put off by failure.

This will ensure that you are in with a fighting chance of getting the job that you want.

Good Luck!

**

Internet sites for jobseekers and CV compilation

https://nationalcareers.service.gov.uk/

The National Careers Service offers CV compilation advice

www.kent.ac.uk/careers/cv/cvexamples.htm

The University of Kent graduate website which is very helpful indeed and offers sound advice in all areas of putting together a CV and also interview tips.

www.myperfectcv.co.uk

A very useful commercial CV website

www.jobsite.co.uk

Offers a CV compilation service

As we have discussed, it is becoming more common to send CV's and also to glean job information over the internet. The below represents some of the best sites.

www.jobstheguardian.com

This site has many new jobs every day. Jobs are sorted by type and it is easy to search for jobs that are relevant to your needs. You can

162

complete a profile on this site to which your CV can be attached. This can then be made available to specific employers who might be in interested in you. There is no charge for this service. You can also upload your CV so that it can be sent to any vacancy advertised.

www.ft.com/recruit

This is the Financial Times Recruitment site, specialising particularly in the financial sector.

www.timesonline.co.uk

This is the website of the Times newspaper group, which contains their job pages. The site includes CV tips and useful guidelines.

www.reed.co.uk

This site is owned by Reed employment who are a well known employment agency. As befits employments agencies, it includes many tips and useful guidance on CV compilation, job searching, interviews etc.

Monster Job Search Online : www.monster.com

Search The Top UK JOBS: www.totaljobs.com

Find Job Vacancies in your Area: www.cv-library.co.uk
www. cv-library.co.uk

Tesco careers Stores.tesco-careers

BBC Careers www.bbc.co.uk/careers

www.careerbuilder.co.uk

Voluntary work sites
www.jobseekers.direct.gov.uk

This is the UK government's main portal to all sorts of jobs, training and volunteering opportunities.

www.jobcentreplus.gov.uk
The UK government's job website.

https://www.ncvo.org.uk/This site is run by volunteering England and usually has many opportunities.

Other general sites
Royal British legion (ex servicemen and women) www.rbli.co.uk

General business directory: www.ukbusinesspark.co.uk

Confederation of British Industry www.cbi.org.uk

****

Index